Growing in Love

Living the gospel of life

PRINCIPAL PROGRAM CONSULTANTS

James J. DeBoy, Jr., MA
Toinette M. Eugene, PhD
Rev. Richard C. Sparks, CSP, PhD

CONSULTANTS

Sr. Jude Fitzpatrick, CHM
Pedagogy

Rev. Mark A. Ressler
Theology

Rev. Douglas O. Wathier
Theology

Daniel J. Bohle, MD (Obstetrics and Gynecology) and Anne Bohle, RN
Family Medicine and Parenting

REVIEWERS

Sr. Connie Carrigan, SSND
Religion Coordinator
Archdiocese of Miami
Miami, Florida

Mark Ciesielski
Associate Director, Office of
Continuing Christian Education
Diocese of Galveston-Houston
Houston, Texas

Margaret Vale DeBoy
Teacher
Arbutus Middle School
Arbutus, Maryland

Diane Dougherty
Director of Children's and
Family Catechesis
Archdiocese of Atlanta
Atlanta, Georgia

Harry J. Dudley, D. Min.
Associate Executive Director
of Faith Formation
Archdiocese of Indianapolis
Indianapolis, Indiana

Steven M. Ellair
Diocesan Consultant for
Elementary Catechesis
Archdiocese of Los Angeles
Los Angeles, California

Kirk Gaddy
Principal
St. Katharine Campus/
Queen of Peace School
Baltimore, Maryland

Connie McGhee
Principal
Most Holy Trinity School
San Jose, California

Barbara Minczewski
Religion Formation
Coordinator
Diocese of Davenport
Davenport, Iowa

Sr. Judy O'Brien, IHM
Rockville Centre, New York

Kenneth E. Ortega
Consultant for Media and
Curriculum
Diocese of Joliet
Joliet, Illinois

Sr. Barbara Scully, SUSC
Assistant Director of Religious
Education
Archdiocese of Boston
Randolph, Massachusetts

Rev. John H. West, STD
Theological Consultant,
Department of Education
Archdiocese of Detroit
Rector, St. John's Center for
Youth and Families
Plymouth, Michigan

Harcourt
Religion Publishers

Nihil Obstat
Rev. Richard L. Schaefer
Censor Deputatus

Imprimatur
✠ Most Rev. Jerome Hanus, OSB
Archbishop of Dubuque
January 28, 2000
Feast of Saint Thomas Aquinas, Patron of Chastity and of Students

The nihil obstat and imprimatur are official declarations that a book or pamphlet is free of doctrinal or moral error. No implication is contained herein that those who granted the nihil obstat and imprimatur agree with the contents, opinions, or statements expressed.

Our Mission
The primary mission of Harcourt Religion Publishers is to provide the Catholic markets with the highest quality catechetical print and media resources. The content of these resources reflects the best insights of current theology, methodology, and pedagogical research. These resources are practical and easy to use, designed to meet expressed market needs, and written to reflect the teachings of the Catholic Church.

Illustration Credits
Articulate Graphics: Joel and Sharon Harris: 8

Photography Credits
Bridgeman Art Libary: *Adam and Eve,* 1955 (w/c, pen and ink on paper), by Marc Chagall (1887–1985) Private Collection: 18; *Portrait of the Artist Watching Her Children Growing* (acrylic on canvas and wood), by P.J. Crook (b. 1945), Cheltenham Art Gallery & Museums, Gloucestershire, UK: 28; *The Woman Taken in Adultery* (panel), by Ortolano (Giovanni B. Benvenuti) (c. 1488–c. 1525), Courtauld Gallery, London, UK: 26; **Gene Plaisted/The Crosiers:** 20; **Digital Imaging Group:** 25, 29, 31; **Jack Holtel:** 21; **Image Bank:** Adeo: 27; **Masterfile:** Mark Tomalty: 24; **Skjold Photographs:** 19; **Tony Stone Images:** Charles Gupton: 22; Bill Truslow: 23; **Unicorn Stock Photos:** Karen Holsinger Mullen: 30

Cover
Photos by **Jack Holtel; The Crosiers**

Printed in the United States of America

ISBN 0-15-950700-6

10 9 8 7 6 5 4 3 2 1

Growing in Love

FAMILY RESOURCE 8

Introduction/Overview 4

Growing in Love at Home 6

Talking with Your Child About . . .

Reproductive Anatomy 8

Natural Family Planning 9

Genital Sexuality and Abuse 10

Pornography and Prostitution 10

Sexual Abuse and Assault 11

Marriage 12

Resolving Family Conflicts 13

Answering Your Child's Questions 14

Additional References 17

HomeLink Pages

Chapter 1   Christian Personhood 18

Chapter 2   Trinity of Love 20

Chapter 3   Living for Others 22

Chapter 4   Communities of Love 24

Chapter 5   God's Life in Us 26

Chapter 6   Life in the Spirit 28

Chapter 7   Our Lifelong Love Story 30

Family Prayers 32

INTRODUCTION AND OVERVIEW

Congratulations!

You have embarked on one of the most exciting adventures of family life—the process of sharing with your child your Catholic values concerning family life, the morality of relationships, and human sexuality. It can be a daunting prospect, especially in today's media-saturated and often values-deprived culture, but no one is better equipped than you to carry out this most important educational task. In this adventure you have the support of your parish community and the whole family of faith that is the Church. The *Growing in Love* program has been developed to help you, in partnership with your faith community, respond to the mandate expressed by popes and bishops, a mandate placed on all of us as members of the human family guided by the Spirit of God:

"The mission to provide education and lifelong learning for ourselves and our children concerning human sexuality is not exhausted by any single program, institution, or approach. By their complementary and cooperative efforts, individuals, parents, families, schools, churches, and the wider society can work together to educate all people about this gift called sexuality. We believe that blending moral and values-based *formation* with clear and factual *information* is the best approach to sexuality education, whether done in the family setting or in more formal programs or some combination of the two" *(Human Sexuality: A Catholic Perspective for Education and Lifelong Learning, p. 83).*

The information on these pages will help introduce you to some of the fundamental principles upon which the *Growing in Love* program is based.

"In a Catholic context, the purpose of . . . education in human sexuality, whether formal or informal, is threefold:

"1. To give each learner an understanding of the nature and importance of sexuality as a divine gift, a fundamental component of personality, and an enrichment of the whole person—body, emotions, soul—whose deepest meaning is to lead the person to the gift of self in love (Cf. *Educational Guidance in Human Love*, nos. 4, 16; *Familiaris Consortio*, nos. 37, 11, 32).

"2. To give each learner an appreciation of chastity as a virtue that develops a person's authentic maturity and makes him or her capable of guiding the sexual instinct in the service of love and integrating it into his or her psychological and spiritual development (Cf. *Educational Guidance*, nos. 4, 18, 34; *Familiaris Consortio*, no. 37).

"3. To give each learner an appreciation of the human and Christian values that sexuality is intended to express and to lead each learner to a knowledge of, respect for, and sincere personal adherence to the moral norms regarding sexuality that are taught by the Church (Cf. *Educational Guidance*, nos. 19, 40; *Familiaris Consortio*, nos. 33, 37)."

(Human Sexuality: A Catholic Perspective for Education and Lifelong Learning, pp. 74–75)

"Four Principles Regarding Information About Sexuality

"1. Each child is a unique and unrepeatable person and must receive individualized formation. . . .

"2. The moral dimension must always be a part of their explanations. . . .

"3. Formation in chastity and timely information regarding sexuality must be provided in the broadest context of education for love. . . .

"4. Parents should provide this information with great delicacy, but clearly and at the appropriate time. . . ."

(The Truth and Meaning of Human Sexuality, #65–75)

The *Growing in Love* Program

Growing in Love has been developed with fidelity to the guidelines for sexuality education presented by Vatican, U.S., and local diocesan offices. The program centers on seven key themes. Each theme is a way of looking at human sexuality, relationships, and family life through the lens of a particular aspect of the Catholic message. The seven themes, which describe each of us as humans, are:
1. Created in God's image
2. Called to communion with God, who is love
3. Incarnational
4. Responsible to one another as members of Christ's Body
5. Called to holiness and wholeness
6. United, faithful, and life-giving
7. Part of the love story of salvation

The seven themes are explored at each level of the program, deepening in the sophistication of the material according to the developmental age of the child.

For Levels 3–8, *Growing in Love* includes the following materials:
- A *Student Text* for each level, containing seven chapters corresponding to the seven program themes and including in-text activities for you and your child to complete at home
- A *Teaching Guide* for each level, with teaching plans and resources for the seven Student Text chapters
- *Teaching Resources* for each level, including classroom materials (blackline masters for activity and resource sheets to extend the chapter content, and Supplementary Lessons for teaching sensitive issues in group situations) and family materials (Family Letters, HomeNotes, and a Program Evaluation)
- This *Family Resource,* available for each level (see overview below)
- *Parish Resources* (program-wide resources including implementation outlines and videos)

Overview of the *Family Resource*

This 32-page booklet contains materials designed to help you share the *Growing in Love* program with your child. In addition to this introduction and overview, the *Family Resource* contains
- *Growing in Love at Home* (pages 6–7): Directions for using the program in three different learning situations and for integrating it into family life.
- *Talking with Your Child About . . .* (pages 8–13): Practical suggestions (including illustrations and diagrams) for sharing sensitive information and topics with your child. The topics covered in this *Family Resource* are those most appropriate to your child's developmental age.
- *Answering Your Child's Questions* (pages 14–17): Suggested answers (including specific language and terminology) for answering questions your child may ask about sensitive topics. The particular questions and answers covered at each level are those most commonly asked by young people. This section also provides a list of additional references for researching other questions and topics.
- *HomeLink* pages (pages 18–31): Two pages of suggestions for exploring each chapter of the Student Text with your child. These pages also contain materials for your own background: a summary of the lesson content, quotes from pertinent Church documents, a One-Minute Scripture Retreat on the lesson theme, definitions of key vocabulary, and additional resources to use at home.
- *Family Prayers* (page 32): Familiar Catholic prayers to use with your child and in your home.

Church Documents on Sexuality and Family Life Education

The following key documents summarize the Church's teaching on important issues of family life, relationships, and sexuality education. These and other Church documents on related issues can be obtained from the United States Catholic Conference (1-800-235-8722; in Washington, D.C., or outside the United States, 202-722-8716; **www.nccbuscc.org**).

Always Our Children: A Pastoral Message to Parents of Homosexual Children and Suggestions for Pastoral Ministers (U.S. Catholic Bishops' Committee on Marriage and Family)

Educational Guidance in Human Love: Outlines for Sex Education (Congregation for Catholic Education)

Faithful for Life: A Moral Reflection (U.S. Catholic Bishops)

Follow the Way of Love: A Pastoral Message of the U.S. Catholic Bishops to Families

The Gospel of Life: On the Value and Inviolability of Human Life (Evangelium Vitae) (Encyclical of John Paul II)

Human Sexuality: A Catholic Perspective for Education and Lifelong Learning (United States Catholic Conference)

In the Service of Life (Instrumentum Laboris) (Pontifical Council for the Family)

Instruction on Respect for Human Life in Its Origin and on the Dignity of Procreation: Replies to Certain Question of the Day (Donum Vitae) (Congregation for the Doctrine of the Faith)

On the Family (Familiaris Consortio) (Apostolic Exhortation of John Paul II)

On the Regulation of Birth (Humanae Vitae) (Encyclical of Paul VI)

Redeemer of Man (Redemptor Hominis) (Encyclical of John Paul II)

Splendor of Truth: Regarding Certain Fundamental Questions of the Church's Moral Teaching (Veritatis Splendor) (Encyclical of John Paul II)

The Truth and Meaning of Human Sexuality: Guidelines for Education Within the Family (Pontifical Council for the Family)

The Vocation and Mission of the Lay Faithful in the Church and the World (Christifideles Laici) (Apostolic Exhortation of John Paul II)

Growing in Love at Home

There are three general scenarios for sharing the material in the *Growing in Love* program. Each of these scenarios is outlined below, with special information about your role as a parent and how you can best make use of the program materials.

If Your Child Is Using *Growing in Love* in Religion Class

Even though your child is learning the *Growing in Love* material in his or her religion class (whether in a Catholic school or parish school of religion), you are still your child's most important teacher of Catholic values and attitudes about family life, relationships, and sexuality. The *Growing in Love* program has been designed with a strong link between the classroom and the home. Family Letters from your child's teacher or catechist summarize what your child is learning in each lesson. Your child will bring home his or her Student Text, each chapter of which contains an in-text activity for you and your child to complete together. The HomeLink box built into the Student Text activity page gives you an opportunity to show that you have discussed the material with your child and offers a means of conveying to your child's teacher any questions or comments you may have.

Your most important tool for carrying out the ministry you share with your child's teacher or catechist is this *Family Resource*. Your child's experience and understanding of the material covered in *Growing in Love* will not be complete if he or she learns only in a classroom setting. The interaction between you and your child when you review the lesson material (using the practical suggestions on the HomeLink pages for each lesson) will support your parenting efforts, lead to greater closeness and communication between you and your child, and strengthen your child's formation in Catholic Christian morality and values.

The *Growing in Love* program has been designed to give you the initiative in discussing certain sensitive topics with your child. The material covered in the reference sections of this *Family Resource (Talking with Your Child About . . . and Answering Your Child's Questions)* is not part of the regular *Growing in Love* curriculum and will not be covered in the classroom without your permission. The reference sections of this *Family Resource* are designed to empower you to share these very important but intimate topics with your child when and how you know best.

Your child's teacher or catechist and other parish ministers are your support team in this partnership. Don't hesitate to ask for additional help in discussing particular topics. As with the whole spectrum of your child's education, *Growing in Love* requires a strong, respectful partnership between the classroom and the home.

If You Are Using *Growing in Love* in a Combined Parent-Child Setting

The partnership between the parish and the home is most obvious when *Growing in Love* is taught in combined parent-child settings. In this model you and your child meet with other parents and children, facilitated by a teacher, catechist, or other parish minister, to cover the material together. This kind of meeting may include any of a number of strategies, including large-group presentation by the facilitator, small-group discussion, and private conversation between parent and child.

Your facilitator will direct you in the use of *Growing in Love* materials. You will be using your child's Student Text in the group meetings or at home. You will most likely be using the HomeLink pages of this *Family Resource* both in the group meetings and as follow-up at home. Because you will be in direct contact with the facilitator, you will not normally receive Family Letters or use the HomeLink box on the Student Text activity pages to communicate questions or comments (though your facilitator may encourage you to do this if you feel more comfortable communicating in writing).

The material covered in the reference sections of this *Family Resource (Talking with Your Child About . . . and Answering Your Child's Questions)* can be handled in a number of ways when the parent-child group model is employed. Your facilitator may introduce some of this more sensitive material in a group session and then encourage you and your child to continue the discussion privately. Or introduction of these topics may be left entirely to your initiative at home with your child, in the setting where you are most comfortable and at the pace you know is best for your child.

An important factor of the group approach is the support you get from other parents who are sharing this material with their children at the same time. The facilitator and other parish ministers can also provide individualized support, though they recognize that you are your child's most important teacher.

If You Are Teaching *Growing in Love* at Home

You may wish to exercise your option to use *Growing in Love* only at home. There are both benefits and drawbacks to this approach, and both have to do with the fact that in a home-based situation you are your child's only teacher. Many parents believe this is the ideal way to communicate information and values of a sensitive nature, and it is perhaps the necessary choice when certain factors (such as language differences, learning disabilities, or traumatic family circumstances) make it inadvisable for your child to cover this material as part of a group (whether in the classroom or in a facilitated parent-child group situation). By limiting your child's exposure to the *Growing in Love* material to the home, however, you lose the benefits of the give-and-take of discussions with peers or other families, as well as the immediate support of a teacher, catechist, or other facilitator. You should be able to rely on your parish for indirect support such as recommendations of additional resources, and ideally you'll be involved in meetings or conferences with your child's regular religion teacher before, during, and after your use of the *Growing in Love* program at home.

If you've determined to be your child's teacher for *Growing in Love,* you can be confident that the program materials offer all you need to give your child an age-appropriate, firm foundation in Catholic values and morality of family life, relationships, and sexuality. This *Family Resource* will be your "teacher's manual" for the program. Use the suggestions on the HomeLink pages to explore with your child each chapter of the Student Text. Refer to the reference sections of this *Family Resource (Talking with Your Child About . . .* and *Answering Your Child's Questions)* to provide deeper background on sensitive topics.

Even if you are not meeting in a parent-child group setting, you may wish to form a partnership with parents of other children your child's age to share experiences and support one another through the process.

Integrating *Growing in Love* into Your Family Life

No matter which setting your family chooses for sharing *Growing in Love,* the following general suggestions can help you integrate this program into your family's everyday life.

- **Make time for *Growing in Love.*** Set aside a regular time to present, discuss, or review lesson content. Add these times to your family calendar along with your other special family notes such as game times, chore schedules, and exercise plans. If you make sharing this material a regular part of your family routine, you will help your child understand that Catholic values about relationships and sexuality are to be fully integrated into your family's life.
- **Make use of "teachable moments."** Don't confine your discussion of *Growing in Love* material to the designated times. Children bring up key topics and questions whenever something in their environment—a news program, a playground discussion, a TV commercial, or a visit from a pregnant relative—triggers them. If you review the material in the reference sections of this *Family Resource* in advance, you'll be better prepared to make use of spontaneous teaching situations. Do not hesitate to challenge incorrect information and immoral situations presented in the media.
- **Reinforce your discussions with examples.** When your child sees a reference to adoption on a TV show, remind him or her of your earlier discussion of that topic. Invite additional discussion or questions.
- **Don't be afraid to say you don't have all the answers.** Your child may ask questions you aren't prepared to answer—either because you truly don't know, or because you need time to frame an answer that's age-appropriate and reflective of your Catholic values. Do get back to your child once you have more information or, if it's appropriate, involve your child in researching the answers with you.
- **Draw on reinforcements.** Grandparents, godparents, older siblings, your child's pediatrician, a neighbor who's a nurse or an uncle who's a family counselor—all these people can help you share with your child insights into *Growing in Love.*
- **Invite God in.** Help your child see the *Growing in Love* material in a prayerful context. If possible, worship together as a family. Add or extend regular family prayer times. Page 32 of this *Family Resource* contains some familiar prayers that can serve as a starting point.

Reproductive Anatomy

Puberty has probably begun to change your child's body and the bodies of his or her classmates in significant ways. This is a good time to review with your child some basic reproductive anatomy. Use the boxed information and diagrams on these pages to guide your discussion.

Here are some helpful tips for you to use when talking with your child:

- **Don't trivialize the discussion.** It might be embarrassing at first, especially for your child, but it is important that he or she understand what is happening to his or her body. It's also important that you share an age-appropriate discussion. This means using the correct biological terms for body parts and functions. You may use simplified or popular terms at your discretion if they help your child better understand, but remind him or her that we don't use slang because it often disrespects or trivializes our understanding of our sexuality.

- **Try to anticipate questions.** Just because your child isn't asking questions doesn't mean he or she understands everything you are saying. Look for clues in your child's expressions that he or she needs a little more clarification or information.

- **Leave the discussion open-ended.** You will never answer all of your child's questions in one sitting. Therefore, it is important that both of you see this as just the beginning of a discussion that will continue for many years.

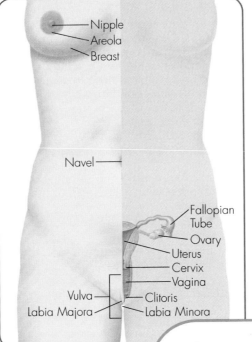

Nipple
Areola
Breast
Navel
Fallopian Tube
Ovary
Uterus
Cervix
Vagina
Vulva
Labia Majora
Clitoris
Labia Minora

The **female reproductive system** is entirely internal. The ovaries, located in the abdomen, produce the hormones estrogen, progesterone, and (in small amounts) testosterone. The ovaries also store and release mature egg cells. About once a month from puberty until menopause, an egg cell *(ovum)* travels into the fallopian tube, where it may be fertilized by a male sperm cell. The fertilized egg then implants itself in the uterus, or *womb.* Sperm cells enter the female body when semen is ejaculated into the vagina, the opening into the woman's body, by the penis during intercourse. Sperm cells travel up through the cervix, the entrance to the uterus, and into the fallopian tubes, aided by muscle contractions that accompany the female's orgasm.

Two sets of fleshy folds, the *labia minora* (inner lips) and *labia majora* (outer lips) surround the entrance to the vagina. The clitoris, located where the labia come together, is composed of erectile tissue and is highly sensitive to stimulation. In females *urine* (liquid waste) leaves the body by the urethra, which opens separately from the vagina. The female breasts produce milk to nourish babies. The nipples are also composed of erectile tissue and are sensitive to stimulation.

Circumcision

Circumcision is the surgical removal of the *foreskin,* the retractable sheath of skin that covers the sensitive glans of the penis. For Jewish males, circumcision (performed in a ritual ceremony called a *bris,* when the infant is eight days old) is required as part of the covenant with God. In our culture in the last fifty years, circumcision has been routinely performed on male babies in the hospital usually the day after birth. However, the health and hygiene benefits of circumcision have recently come into question, and more and more non-Jewish parents are choosing to forgo circumcision for their infant sons. There is no difference in erectile function between a circumcised and an uncircumcised penis. When the foreskin is left intact, boys must be instructed in retracting the foreskin and keeping the area under it clean and free from bacteria.

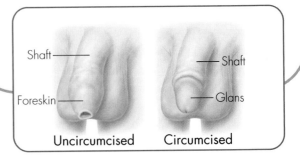

Shaft
Foreskin
Shaft
Glans
Uncircumcised   Circumcised

The **male reproductive system** has both internal and external organs. The testes, two glands located outside the body in the pouch called the scrotum, produce the hormone testosterone. At puberty the testes begin producing sperm cells. Sperm cells are stored inside the body in the epididymus until they mature. When the penis, the external reproductive organ located in front of the scrotum, is stimulated, it becomes firm and erect. This stimulation causes sperm cells to move through the seminal vesicle to the vas deferens, where they are mixed with a fluid called *semen* from the prostate gland and Cowper's glands. At orgasm semen is ejaculated through the urethra, which leads through the penis to an opening in the *glans*, or tip. Urine is also carried out of the body through the urethra, but during ejaculation urine is prevented from mingling with the semen. The male breasts do not manufacture milk, but the male nipples are composed of erectile tissue and may be sensitive to stimulation.

Natural Family
Planning

When discussing Natural Family Planning with your child, it is important to remind him or her that the purpose of marriage, according to the Church, is twofold: it is life-giving and love-giving. Sexual intercourse lovingly unifies the couple and is, by nature, open to the possibility of conceiving a child.

In some situations, though, there may be legitimate reasons—certain health conditions, for example, or the lack of resources for responsible parenting—why a married couple would want to defer or avoid conceiving a child. In contrast to much of society, which promotes the use of artificial methods of birth control, the Church teaches that family planning must be carried out responsibly and naturally. Here are some points for discussing Natural Family Planning with your child:

- **Natural Family Planning is the combination of methods** approved by the Church for the responsible spacing of births.

- **By attuning themselves to the wife's individual fertility cycle,** a married couple can identify the timespan surrounding ovulation during which conception would be most likely to occur. If the couple wish to conceive a child, they can engage in sexual intercourse at the most favorable time. If they wish to postpone conception, they can practice abstinence from sexual intercourse during the fertile period.

- **Observation of such natural signs** as a rise in the woman's body temperature and changes in the consistency of cervical mucus allow the couple to accurately time ovulation. If these changes are charted on a calendar over a period of months, the woman's times of fertility and infertility can be determined, and conception can be accurately and naturally planned or deferred.

- **Married couples who make use of Natural Family Planning** often find that intimacy is increased by their consciousness of the fertility cycle and by the freedom to develop a wide range of expressions of love during periods of abstinence.

Genital Sexuality and Abuse

Have you ever been in such a hurry to get somewhere that you decide to take a shortcut? The next thing you know, you're lost or in a worse spot than before. The genital expression of sexuality is a lot like that. It's a shortcut to love. Often, in a couple's eagerness to get to love and intimacy, they head in the wrong direction. As Catholics we believe that the best course is to wait until we are in a committed, married relationship before we engage in genital sexuality.

Your child will more than likely hear messages from his or her peers, or from the media, that trivialize genital sexuality.

Misconceptions About Sexuality

Here are some common misconceptions and suggestions for dealing with false messages:

- **"Masturbation and oral or anal sex are less dangerous than sexual intercourse and therefore acceptable behavior for teens."** People think that just because an action doesn't involve the opportunity for a pregnancy, it's acceptable. First of all, the Catholic Church teaches that the only relationship in which genital sexuality is appropriate is that of a married couple. Second, couples who engage in oral and anal sex still risk the transfer of sexually transmitted diseases, so it is certainly not safe.

- **"The Church is just being old-fashioned."** If we gauge what is morally acceptable from many of the messages of television programs or movies, adultery and premarital sex have indeed become more acceptable and common. But explain to your child that the media have a priority that is different from ours. Their job is to sell a product, and sex sells. The media is constantly trying to exploit our weaknesses as consumers, whether it's convincing us that we need to have a perfect body to be socially acceptable, or whether it's feeding our sexual urges to sell us movies or perfume. Sometimes we need to take a step back from the barrage of messages to sort the hype from the things that really matter to us.

Pornography and Prostitution

Pornography and prostitution flow from selfish views of sexuality that harm the dignity of the human person, demean the gift of sexuality that God has given us, and erode the trust within a marriage or family.

Pornography is sexually explicit material in magazines, videos, CDs, and other media that demeans or trivializes God's gift. Pornography that uses children is especially harmful. Pornography is particularly dangerous to teens because it gives them the wrong messages about their sexuality during a formative time in their development. It is easy for children and teens to access pornography through the Internet. Teach your child to be careful and conscientious on-line.

Prostitution, like pornography, is a business that exploits sexuality for a profit. And like pornography, prostitution is often seen as victimless. But there are victims. The prostitute, whether male or female, rarely makes the free choice to sell his or her body, and in many situations is either physically or emotionally abused by the customer or pimp. The customer, having chosen to engage in premarital or extramarital sexual activity, is putting himself or herself and his or her family (or future family) at risk of contracting a sexually transmitted disease. By choosing to use a prostitute, the customer is also disrespecting the relationship he or she has (or will have) with his or her spouse.

So what can you do to protect your child from the harmful effects of pornography and prostitution?

- **Teach your child that it is wrong to treat another person as an object.** The only time sexual intimacy is appropriate is when it is shared within a loving, married relationship. Any other time sexual intimacy is a means for selfish gratification and is morally wrong.

- **You need to be the primary source of your child's information on sexuality.** Often teens use pornography to answer questions they have about sexuality. If your child feels comfortable coming to you to answer any of his or her questions about sexuality, he or she will be less likely to use harmful sources to get the information.

- **Explain that the exploitation of sex as a business is not victimless.** Everyone involved is hurt in one way or another when someone chooses to misuse his or her sexuality.

Sexual Abuse and Assault

Sexual assault and abuse are difficult to discuss, and it's very hard to imagine our children as victims of these terrible crimes. Yet sexual assault and abuse occur at all levels of society, in all parts of the world. No one is immune. Sadly, many times the perpetrator is known to or even related to the victim.

You can help your child by presenting candid, factual information about rape and sexual abuse. Without unduly frightening your child, talk over what to do in threatening situations. Let your child know that you will *always* listen to his or her concerns.

Rape

- Rape is forcible sexual assault, causing someone to have oral, anal, or vaginal intercourse against his or her will. The force can be physical (hitting, restraining, or using a weapon) or psychological (threats, manipulative comments). Rape also describes having sexual relations with a person who is too drugged or drunk to give consent.

- Rape is *never* provoked or justified by the appearance or actions of the victim.

- Rape is committed against both males and females.

- Many victims of rape know the perpetrator. This is called *date rape* or *acquaintance rape*.

- In some parts of the country, even consensual sex with someone under a certain age is considered rape by the civil law.

Sexual Abuse

- Sexual abuse is any sexual contact by an adult with a child or between two adults when one is in a position to exercise power over the other (such as a teacher and a student or a supervisor and an employee).

- Examples of sexual abuse include touching or fondling the genitals; having oral, anal, or vaginal sexual relations with a child; and exhibitionism *(flashing)*.

- Incest is a form of sexual abuse. Incest is sexual contact between biological, adoptive, or foster family members, such as might occur between an adult family member and child or between siblings.

- The effects of incest and other forms of sexual abuse are long-lasting because the very person who was entrusted to love and protect the child has violated him or her.

Helping an Abused or Sexually Assaulted Child

- **Get medical and law-enforcement assistance.** Calmly find out what happened, and explain that you will tell only those who need to know in order to help. Make sure the child gets proper medical attention. Whether it's physical abuse or a sexual assault, a doctor can better assess what treatment the child might need. The doctor will also be able to document the incident. When you are sure the child is safe, you should also contact either the police or child protective services.

- **Help the child through the emotional trauma.** It's hard to trust anyone after being abused, especially after being sexually abused. But the child needs your help. Abused children will feel afraid, guilty, and depressed. Reassure the child that he or she shouldn't feel guilty about what happened, and reaffirm your continued love and support. Families torn apart by incest or child abuse must learn how to stop the abuse and how to rebuild the trust and love within the family. Often this takes the involvement of a professional counselor.

- **Restore the child's faith in God.** Faith can heal and restore. Remind the child that God wants him or her to be safe, happy, and loved. Victims can have trouble trusting God, because they often blame him for not stopping the abuse. If need be, meet with a parish staff member to talk about things you can do to help affirm the child's relationship with God.

Marriage

As Catholics we believe that marriage is a sacrament and a way of life—it is a covenant of love. The couple mutually pledges to commit themselves to each other for life. In this sacrament of God's love for us, a man and a woman give themselves completely to each other in a life-giving and unselfish covenant of mutual love and commitment. Sexual intercourse is an expression both of the couple's love for each other and of their willingness to have children. In the eyes of God and the Church, a sacramental marriage lasts until the death of one of the spouses.

Our society tends to be pessimistic about marriage, using the high-profile breakups of celebrities and the rising divorce rates as evidence that relationships just don't last. But a committed, loving marriage usually is one of the most fulfilling and joyful experiences in a person's life. Having a partner who can celebrate your joys and share your concerns is both rewarding and comforting. Within a marriage a couple can also share in one of the highest forms of love for one another through the birth or adoption of a child.

Yet we all know that marriages do not always meet these important expectations. Relationships aren't always easy. People change over time. And while some grow closer, others grow apart. Half of all first marriages fail, so it is very likely that your child will be faced with the breakup of a family close to him or her. Here are some suggestions and clarifications to help discuss the different situations:

- **Even if the breakup is not in your family,** the child may become extra sensitive to the relationships of people close to him or her. Reassure your child that your family relationships are still strong, and encourage him or her to talk about concerns he or she has.

- **If the breakup is in your own family,** carefully talk though the issues surrounding the situation, and encourage your child to ask questions. He or she will likely be very confused, so it is important to establish and maintain the lines of communication.

- **Be careful not to place blame.** If possible, don't place all blame on one person or the other. Try to be fair to the situation.

After the Breakup of a Marriage

- **Divorce.** The Catholic Church does not believe that human power can end a sacramental marriage, but many Catholic couples do choose to end the legal aspect of their marriages through civil divorce. A civil divorce usually involves a division of property and establishes terms regarding finances and children. Often it is preceded by a legal **separation,** which is a period of time assigned by the courts for the couple to reevaluate their decision. If, after the required time, the couple wants to continue divorce proceedings, the court hears the case. In a civil divorce the Church recognizes the couple's need to protect their legal rights, but if the marriage was sacramental, the sacramental nature of their marriage remains intact. Divorced and separated people are not excommunicated. They may fully participate in the Church community, including the Eucharist, if they do not remarry or if they obtain an annulment before they remarry.

- **Declaration of nullity (annulment).** An annulment is a formal declaration by the Church that a sacramental marriage never existed. It doesn't sever the civil marriage bonds or answer legal questions about property, finances, or the custody of the children. If the marriage was legal, the children are legitimate. An annulment is simply a declaration that the sacramental reality of the marriage was null or invalid from the beginning. Perhaps the partners did not freely consent because of psychological immaturity, or maybe they never intended to create a sacramental marriage or one never intended to have children.

Resolving
Family Conflicts

We all have family conflicts. Some are more serious than others, but how we deal with family conflicts is important to our emotional well-being as a family.

In some families conflicts can become violent. Domestic violence is a serious problem and one that is sometimes well hidden and difficult to acknowledge and deal with. The violence can take the form of battering a spouse (either male or female) or a child, or it can be psychological or sexual. Domestic violence is as dangerous when it is emotional or verbal as it is when it is physical. The abuser may not plan to hurt others and may deny what happened later or promise that the incident will not be repeated. He or she may even blame the victim. None of these strategies excuses or mitigates the action or diminishes the need to deal with the situation.

Family violence can take on many different forms. Here are a few:

- *physical assault*—including pushing, hitting, kicking, biting, choking, or using a weapon
- *forced sexual contact and rape*
- *destruction of property*
- *injury or destruction of pets*
- *threats and intimidation*—including threats to harm children or other family members
- *excessive control of the victim*—including control of money, transportation, activities, and social contacts
- *psychological control*—berating and demeaning the victim to destroy self-esteem

If domestic violence toward you or your child is occurring, it is important that you call the appropriate authorities. If you are concerned for your safety, many organizations allow you to place your report anonymously and provide a safe place for you and your children.

Domestic violence is hard to change. The cycle of abuse usually repeats itself unless someone intervenes. Victims desperately want to believe it was a onetime occurrence or focus only on the positive qualities of the perpetrator. But victims of domestic abuse need to develop the self-confidence to admit the abuse and the courage to break out of the relationship if the abuse continues, even if the relationship is a marriage. Here are some suggestions that you can use when talking with your child about domestic violence:

Countering Violence

- **Work to avoid violence in your own life.** Unfortunately, violence is very real in our society. Explain to your child that every time we stereotype people, say hurtful things to family or friends, or treat others with anger and disrespect, we may be tending toward violence. We can't work credibly to change the actions of others unless we can also control ourselves.

- **Do your part to stop the causes of violence.** Confront unfairness, prejudice, and hatred when you see it. Teach your child to see each side of an argument and to work for just solutions.

- **Take domestic violence seriously.** Domestic violence injures and even kills people. Your child should know that under no circumstance is domestic abuse to be tolerated and that there are people who can help and laws that provide protection. Teachers, health professionals, and others are required by law to report child abuse. In many states police are required to follow up on any instance of domestic violence. This sometimes means that a restraining order is initiated for a period of time. If you or your child suspects domestic violence in another family, the violence can be reported anonymously if you choose, but it should be reported.

- **Let your faith help you.** The U.S. Bishops condemn domestic violence and those who use selected passages from the Bible to condone abusive attitudes or behaviors *(When I Call for Help: Domestic Violence Against Women)*. Jesus reached out to heal those who were hurting, not to judge them. He respected the dignity of all people, especially those who were most vulnerable. He is there to do the same for those who are abused, trapped, and hurting today.

Answering Your Child's Questions

Here are some questions young teens may ask about sexuality, along with some suggested answers. Occasionally this section will treat topics that are unlikely to arise, but because of our culture they may. You may not want to initiate discussion of these topics, but you should be prepared to respond to questions from your child. Should you choose to discuss these topics with your child, you may find this background material helpful. Explain only as much of this information as your child seems to want to know. Be sensitive to your child's age and level of maturity when choosing appropriate information to share.

What does "losing your virginity" mean? What is "secondary virginity"?

A virgin is a person who has not engaged in sexual intercourse. "Losing your virginity" is a popular expression for having sexual intercourse for the first time. There is no way to tell whether a person is a virgin. In girls who have not yet had sexual intercourse, a thin membrane called the hymen partially covers the opening to the vagina. (The hymen allows the menstrual flow to leave the vagina, and in most girls it allows the insertion of a tampon.) However, the hymen can be perforated by many activities besides intercourse, including horseback riding and other vigorous exercise, so its absence is not proof of sexual activity. A woman whose hymen remains intact until her first experience of sexual intercourse may experience some discomfort and slight bleeding when the penis is inserted, but feelings of sexual pleasure and excitement (especially if the experience takes place within a caring and committed relationship) compensate for the discomfort. The Church's teaching on reserving sexual intercourse for marriage promotes making the first sexual experience a deeply personal gift of oneself in loving intimacy.

Some people believe that engaging in sexual activities other than intercourse (such as oral or anal sex, whether heterosexual or homosexual) outside of marriage is okay because these activities don't "technically" violate virginity. But being a virgin is not just a technical or physical state. Intimate sexual activity, even if it does not include intercourse, is reserved for the committed union of a man and woman in marriage. A person who is the victim of a sexual assault or molestation remains a virgin regardless of his or her physical experience, because the self-giving for which sexual intimacy was designed did not occur.

So-called "secondary virginity" is a voluntary promise, made by a person who has been sexually active prematurely, to abstain from sexual intercourse until marriage. Many young people find it difficult to withstand the pressure from peers and society to become sexually active at an early age. Or they may be so driven by curiosity about the mystery of sexuality that they experiment. These actions are morally wrong. People who engage in premarital sex risk pregnancy or STD infection. But people are capable of changing their lives for the better. It takes courage to turn your life around, but restoring God's great gift of sexual intimacy to its rightful place within marriage is worth the effort.

How will I know when I've found the right person to marry if I haven't had any sexual experiences?

There are many factors involved in achieving a successful marriage. Many studies have shown that so-called "sexual compatibility" is one of the least important of these factors. If a couple share friendship, loyalty, similar values, and have taken the time to get to know one another well enough to make a lifelong commitment, then the love and sexual attraction they feel for one another will find expression in married sexual intimacy. Dating should be practice in real love and lasting relationship skills, not lovemaking. Sexual involvement and promiscuity before marriage can actually have negative effects on marriages (not to mention the heightened risks of teen pregnancy and STDs). Statistics show that couples who live together before marriage are at a higher risk for separation and divorce than those who reserve sexual intimacy for marriage.

What is impotence? Is there a corresponding problem for women?

Impotence, or erectile dysfunction, in men is the temporary or permanent inability to sustain an erection. Impotence may have many causes, whether physical (such as nerve damage or medications that affect circulation) or emotional (such as depression or unexpressed anger toward the partner). Fatigue, stress, alcohol and drug use, smoking, and age can all affect potency. Most cases of erectile dysfunction, which prevents sexual intimacy and affects fertility, can be helped with surgery, medication, behavior modification (such as quitting smoking), or counseling.

There is no corresponding condition for women. However, many physical and emotional factors can affect whether a woman's body responds to sexual intimacy in a pleasurable way. If a woman is stressed, tired, or ill, for example, her vagina may not become lubricated and she may find intercourse irritating or painful. Many women also find orgasm difficult to achieve without direct stimulation of the clitoris.

What is anal sex?

Anal sex involves the use of the penis, tongue, lips, fingers, or some other object to stimulate the sensitive area around and inside the anus and rectum. Anal sex, while popularly associated with gay men, is sometimes practiced by heterosexual couples and lesbians. Some heterosexual young people believe that anal sex is a harmless substitute for intercourse. However, anal sex carries very high risks of physical injury, infection, and transmission of STDs, especially the HIV virus. Any practice of anal sex outside of consensual use as part of foreplay (preparation for vaginal intercourse) by a married couple is a grave misuse of the gift of sexuality and is therefore sinful.

What are "sex toys"? What is "S and M"?

So-called "sex toys" are objects used to stimulate the genitals in individual or mutual masturbation. You may have heard references to a *dildo,* or artificial penis, for example, or to the use of a vibrator to massage the genitals. Any artificial devices may only add another layer of dehumanization to masturbation, which in itself separates sexual activity from its God-given meaning. "S and M" stands for sexual practices that rely for sexual gratification on *sadism* (the need to inflict pain and humiliation on others) and *masochism* (the need to experience humiliation and pain).

In adults, these and other nontraditional sexual practices, such as *voyeurism* (sexual gratification from spying on others), *exhibitionism* (sexual gratification from exposing one's genitals in public), *bestiality* (sexual activity with animals) and *fetishism* (sexual gratification linked to touching or wearing certain objects) are usually signs of emotional immaturity and may lead to psychological problems or criminal behavior. Experimenting with any of these practices is wrong.

What's a "test tube baby"? What's a "surrogate mother"?

Both of these terms refer to extraordinary methods of conceiving or carrying a child—meaning methods outside the normal processes of conception and pregnancy. A "test tube baby" is a child conceived through *in vitro* fertilization, a process by which the mother's egg and the father's sperm are extracted and joined to each other under laboratory conditions in a test tube or petri dish. The fertilized ovum is then implanted into the mother's uterus. Sometimes many eggs are fertilized and only one or a few are implanted. The so-called "surplus" embryos may be frozen for later use or destroyed. If more than one embryo begins to grow in the woman's body, she may choose to have some removed through abortion and allow only the most desirable number to survive. A "surrogate mother" is a woman who has another couple's fertilized ovum implanted in her uterus, where the child grows until birth and is then given to the biological parents.

These and some other technological means developed to help couples overcome fertility problems are morally wrong, both because they interfere with God's plan for the unitive and procreative dimensions of human sexuality and because they almost always lead to the destruction of embryos, which is the taking of innocent human life. However, there are medical procedures for enhancing fertility (such as prescribing fertility drugs or hormones) and increasing the possibility of conception (such as the GIFT procedure, in which a fertilized egg is surgically assisted in becoming implanted) that do not interfere with the marital act or involve the death of embryos. These techniques are not forbidden by the Church. In any case, we believe that every human life is precious, no matter how the child was conceived or carried to birth.

Is celibacy possible?

Yes, the Church has always taught that voluntarily abstaining from marriage and sexual intimacy is a special gift that requires the support of a strong friendship with God, mature friendships with others, and a healthy sense of self-esteem. The sexual urge is very strong, but it is not on the same level as hunger or thirst. Abstaining from sexual intercourse does not cause physical or emotional harm. Adults who are single by choice or circumstance, priests, members of religious communities, and those who are of a homosexual orientation are capable of abstaining from sexual intercourse and living fulfilled, loving lives.

Do married people outgrow the desire for sexual intimacy?

No. Although the hormones that contribute to sexual desire are at their peak during the childbearing years of young adulthood, humans desire and are capable of sexual intimacy throughout their adult lives. Once she has passed menopause, a woman can no longer conceive a child, but a man continues to produce sperm and is theoretically capable of fathering a child at even an advanced age. Married couples may engage in sexual intercourse less frequently as they grow older, but as long as they remain otherwise healthy, intercourse and other physical expressions of intimacy remain an important way for older couples to share love and closeness.

Why is it wrong to have an extramarital affair?

Studies show that adultery does emotional and spiritual harm to everyone involved. It violates the public commitment a husband and wife have made to each other, and thus is a grave sin. The spouse and children of the partner involved in an extramarital affair have had their trust violated and have been deprived of the love and intimacy that is rightfully theirs.

The cheating spouse may feel an initial boost from having been found attractive by another person, but must live an increasingly dishonest life. The person having an affair with a married person sacrifices his or her self-esteem and often winds up feeling lonelier than if he or she were not in a relationship at all. Adultery also carries the risk of physical harm through sexually transmitted diseases, which may infect the innocent spouse as well. There is also the risk of pregnancy outside the marriage.

Adultery does not have to destroy a marriage, but overcoming the damage done by an extramarital affair takes strong faith and often counseling for all involved, as well as a serious commitment to identify and work through the hurt that has been experienced.

These resources may help you answer further questions and continue to talk with your child about sexuality and Catholic values. Some resources listed below are rooted in other Christian traditions and will need to be adapted for Catholic families or supplemented with specifically Catholic teaching.

Before You Were Born, by Henry O'Brien and Joan Lowery Nixon (Our Sunday Visitor, 1980).

A beautifully illustrated reflection on the miracle of pregnancy and birth, simple enough for young children but useful for all ages. (K–3)

Catholic Sexual Ethics, by Ronald Lawler, Joseph Boyle Jr., and William E. May (Our Sunday Visitor, 1998).

A sourcebook on Catholic teaching about sexuality issues. (Adult)

Contemporary Christian Morality, by Richard C. Sparks (Crossroad Publishing, 1996).

One hundred of the most frequently asked questions regarding moral issues answered from a Christian viewpoint. (Adult)

How and When to Tell Your Kids About Sex: A Lifelong Approach to Shaping Your Child's Sexual Character, by Stanton L. Jones and Brenna B. Jones (Navarre Press, 1993).

This guide comes from an evangelical Christian point of view and does not provide the nuances of Catholic teaching, but it offers parents of all Christian backgrounds a practical and positive approach. (Adult)

How to Talk Confidently with Your Child About Sex . . . And Appreciate Your Own Sexuality, Too, by Lenore Buth (Concordia Publishing House, 1995).

Practical advice from a Christian perspective. (Adult)

How You Were Born, by Joanna Cole (Morrow Junior Books, 1993).

An exploration of the beautiful process of childbirth. (K–3)

Know Your Body: A Family Guide to Sexuality and Fertility, by Charles Norris and Jean Weibel Owen (Our Sunday Visitor, 1982).

Written from a faithful Catholic perspective, this guide is particularly helpful for discussing Natural Family Planning. (Adult)

Sex Education for Toddlers to Young Adults, by James Kenny (St. Anthony Messenger Press, 1989).

A straight-talking guide for parents regarding many pertinent topics. (Adult)

Sex Is Not a Four-Letter Word! by Patricia Martens Miller (Crossroad Publishing, 1994).

Practical suggestions for age-appropriate discussions between parents and children regarding sex. (Adult)

Sex Is More than a Plumbing Lesson, by Patty Stark (Preston Hollow Enterprises, 1991).

Encourages parents to share their values and beliefs regarding sexuality with their own children in age-appropriate ways. (Adult)

Tender Love: God's Gift of Sexual Intimacy, by Bill Hybels and Rob Wilkins (Moody Press, 1993).

A look at the spiritual side of sexuality and commitment in marriage as necessary to love in a fully human way. (Adult)

Harcourt Religion Publishers Multimedia Resources

Catholic Values and Sexuality (video).

Sixteen significant topics covered through drama and documentary; Parent Guide available. (Jr. High–Adult)

God's Gift (video) (produced by the Archdiocese of St. Paul-Minneapolis).

Six videos on sexuality topics, geared to children's level of understanding. (K–6)

Growing in Love (video).

Explores program themes and gives parents background in sharing this material with their children. (Adult)

Marriage (video) (produced by Golden Dome Productions).

Four videos explore all stages and aspects of married life. (High School–Adult)

Movie and Video Reviews
For ratings and reviews of current and previously released films, call the toll-free hotline sponsored by the United States Catholic Conference's Office for Film and Broadcasting. The number is **1-800-311-4CCC.** You may also find selected movie and video reviews and other media information at the Web site of the Catholic Communications Campaign **(www.nccbuscc.org/ccc).**

Christian Personhood

The Teaching Church

"The Christian tradition has also understood this passage [Genesis] as illustrating a natural mutuality and equality that exist between man and woman. 'The sexes are complementary: similar and dissimilar at the same time; not identical, the same, though, in dignity of person; they are peers so that they may mutually understand each other, diverse in their reciprocal completion.' *(Educational Guidance in Human Love, no. 25; See also Familiaris Consortio, no. 22.)* Both man and woman are *persons*—equal yet distinct" *(Human Sexuality: A Catholic Perspective for Education and Lifelong Learning, p. 8).*

One-Minute Scripture Retreat

Read

But you are "a chosen race, a royal priesthood, a holy nation, a people of his own, so that you may announce the praises" of him who called you out of darkness into his wonderful light.

—1 Peter 2:9

Reflect

How has my self-image been shaped? How do I affect the self-image of my friends and family? How do I understand myself as a holy person and a member of a royal priesthood?

_____

_____

Getting Started

Watch a half hour of television with your child. Make a list of messages about physical appearance that you observe within that half hour. Discuss how realistic the messages are.

Ask your child to write a description of himself or herself. Write your own description of your child. Compare your descriptions.

Building Understanding

Ask your child which of the fruits of the Spirit that are listed on page 6 of his or her book he or she best expresses. Ask your child how he or she expresses these qualities.

With your child, read *Catholics Believe* from page 7 of his or her book. Review with your child the differences in male and female anatomy. See pages 8 and 9 of this *Family Resource* for more information on reproductive anatomy.

With your child, review page 7 of his or her book in order to begin a discussion of gender roles and sex discrimination. For more information on gender roles, see page 9 of this *Family Resource*.

Continuing to Grow

With your child, review or complete the activity on page 10 of your child's book.

Find a hinged picture frame that holds two pictures. Put a mirror in one side of the frame. Ask your child to make a copy of the reflection on page 11 of his or her book. Put the copy in the other side of the frame. Display the frame in a place where your family members will see it often.

Together, look back through Chapter 1 of your child's book. Be sure to initial the HomeLink box on page 10 to show that you've reviewed the chapter, and list any comments or questions you may have.

Read and discuss *Keep On Growing* on pages 12 and 13 with your child.

Words from This Chapter

self-image *(p. 4):* The way we see ourselves.

masculinity *(p. 7):* Qualities (sometimes stereotypes) associated with the male gender.

femininity *(p. 7):* Qualities (sometimes stereotypes) associated with the female gender.

eating disorder *(p. 9):* A harmful pattern of physical habits and psychological attitudes associated with eating, often connected with a distorted body image; examples include anorexia and bulimia.

More to Share

Books

For Children

Building Self-Esteem: A Workbook for Teens, by Jerome Trahey (Resource Publications, 1992).

Gives teens practical exercises that can help them find out who they are, what they value, and where they are going in light of gospel messages.

For Adults

Talk with Teens about Self and Stress: 50 Guided Discussions for School and Counseling Groups, by Jean Sunde Peterson (Free Spirit Publishing, 1993).

Guided discussions that help teens make better choices, solve problems, and find confidence in themselves.

Chapter 2

Trinity of Love

Chapter Summary

- God—Father, Son, and Holy Spirit—is love.
- Humans were created for eternal beatitude.
- The virtues of faith, hope, and love are gifts from God that help us grow in love.

The Teaching Church

"Christian theology has long reflected on the revelation of God as a communion of persons, the Trinity. God's inner life is a life of radical sharing and communication among the Father, Son, and Holy Spirit. It is in, through, and out of that mysterious love within God that all life and love come. Created in God's own image, we find inscribed in our hearts one core universal vocation, that is, to love and to be loved. (Cf. *Pastoral Constitution on the Church in the Modern World,* no. 12; *Familiaris Consortio,* no. 11) Love is our origin; love is our constant calling on earth; and love will be our fulfillment in heaven" (Cf. "Wedding Preface III," The Roman Missal) *(Human Sexuality: A Catholic Perspective for Education and Lifelong Learning, p. 7).*

One-Minute Scripture Retreat

Read   *So faith, hope, love remain, these three; but the greatest of these is love.*

—1 Corinthians 13:13

Reflect   When in my life have I been most open to the virtues of faith, hope, and love?

_____

_____

Getting Started

Ask your child to talk about the give-and-take that is part of your family's relationship.

Talk with your child about what kinds of ups and downs he or she expects to face within the next year. Discuss with your child how to prepare for foreseeable successes and disappointments.

Building Understanding

Which of the three theological virtues named on page 16 of your child's book do you need the most? Share your answer with your child. Ask your child which theological virtue he or she needs to grow in the most at this time.

Discuss with your child ways that your family can put faith in action, live in hope, and perform works of love.

Talk with your child about the issues discussed on pages 18 and 19. Suicide and school violence are both important topics, but be sure to end your discussion by focusing on the positive qualities of the virtues mentioned in the final paragraph on page 19.

Continuing to Grow

With your child, review or complete the activity on page 20 of your child's book. Talk with him or her about ways we can communicate to friends who need our help.

Read to your family the reflection on page 21 of your child's book. Ask everyone to find a selection of music that expresses love and joy. Together, listen to each person's selection.

Together, look back through Chapter 2 of your child's book. Be sure to initial the HomeLink box on page 20 to show that you've reviewed the chapter, and list any comments or questions you may have.

Read and discuss *Keep On Growing* on pages 22 and 23 with your child.

Words from This Chapter

theological virtues *(p. 16):* Faith, hope, and love; the three great gifts from God that help us live in relationship with him.

More to Share

Books

For Children

The Power to Prevent Suicide: A Guide for Teens Helping Teens, by Richard E. Nelson Ph.D. and Judith C. Galas (Free Spirit Publishing, 1994).

Provides positive step-by-step advice on how young people can prevent suicide.

For Adults

Talking to Your Children About Being Catholic, by Peter Kreeft, *et al.* (Our Sunday Visitor, 1995).

A collection of writers explain vital components of the Catholic faith to children.

Chapter 3

Living for Others

Chapter Summary

- Friendships help us grow in love.
- Jesus taught us how to live for others.
- There are appropriate ways to express affection and love in friendships and dating.

The Teaching Church

"*Friendships* are very important in this period. According to local social conditions and customs, adolescence is a time when young people enjoy more autonomy in their relations with others and in the hours they keep in family life. Without taking away their rightful autonomy, when necessary, parents should know how to say 'no' to their children and, at the same time, they should know how to cultivate a taste in their children for what is beautiful, noble and true. Parents should also be sensitive to adolescents' self-esteem, which may pass through a confused phase when they are not clear about what personal dignity means and requires" *(The Truth and Meaning of Human Sexuality, #107).*

One-Minute Scripture Retreat

Read

"And the king will say to them in reply, 'Amen, I say to you, whatever you did for one of these least brothers of mine, you did for me.'"

—Matthew 25:40

Reflect

Jesus is our model for perfect love. Which of my relationships best represent perfect love? How do I show that I value these relationships?

_____

_____

Getting Started

Share with your child some of the childish behaviors that you've seen him or her outgrow. Ask your child how he or she has become less self-centered and more other-centered.

Help your child make lists of the risks and benefits of friendships. Use the lists to talk about ways to choose friends and build healthy friendships.

Building Understanding

Discuss with your child healthy boundaries for different kinds of relationships. Explain your own expectations about how your child spends time with his or her friends.

Talk with your child about the ways that people express their sexuality. For more information on abuses of genital sexuality, see page 10 of this *Family Resource*.

With your child, review pages 28 and 29 of the student book. Discuss the different vocations mentioned and the types of affection appropriate to each.

Continuing to Grow

With your child, review or complete the activity on page 30 of your child's book. Talk about some of the qualities in your important friendships and those of your child.

Read the reflection on page 31 with your child. Talk about things you do when you feel overwhelmed at work or at home. Ask your child to share his or her methods. If there is a specific symbol, picture, or item you can use to represent your examples, create and exchange the one that best illustrates your choice.

Together, look back through Chapter 3 of your child's book. Be sure to initial the HomeLink box on page 30 to show that you've reviewed the chapter, and list any questions you may have.

Read and discuss *Keep On Growing* on pages 32 and 33 with your child.

Words from This Chapter

purity *(p. 26):* The virtue that helps us respect our bodies and the bodies of others as temples of the Holy Spirit.

modesty *(p. 26):* The virtue that protects privacy; avoiding extremes of emotion, action, dress, and language.

chastity *(p. 26):* The virtue that helps a person express sexuality appropriately according to his or her vocation.

sexuality *(p. 27):* The ways in which we live (physically, mentally, emotionally, spiritually) as gendered persons, male or female.

abortion *(p. 29):* The death of an unborn baby; *spontaneous abortion,* or *miscarriage,* occurs when the unborn baby dies of natural causes; *direct abortion,* any intentional action taken purposely to cause the death of the unborn baby, is a serious sin.

More to Share

Books

For Children

Responsible Sex, by Jim Auer (Liguori, 1996).

This work presents a Christian view that honors the whole person and offers realistic ways for teens to incorporate this vision into their lives.

For Adults

Between Fathers & Sons, by Michael Smith SJ (Ave Maria Press, 1999).

A gospel-based process for a variety of settings.

Covenant of Love: Pope John Paul II on Sexuality, Marriage, and Family in the Modern World, by Fr. Richard Hogan and Fr. John Le Voir (Ignatius Press, 1992).

Presents Pope John Paul II's vision of the dignity and rights of the person and the importance of the family.

Chapter 4

Communities of Love

Chapter Summary

- The family is the domestic Church.
- Religious life and the priesthood are vocations to love.
- Single life is also a vocation to love.

The Teaching Church

"Genuine love does not promise constant enjoyment, pleasure, and happiness. While hoping for a measure of reciprocity, some degree of mutuality in love relationships, a person whose love is true is willing to go the extra mile, to turn the other cheek, to be committed in bad times as well as good. (Cf. Matthew 5:38–42; see also "Rite of Marriage," *The Roman Ritual*.) Self-giving and sacrifice, fidelity, courage, patience, kindness, forgiveness, hope, perseverance—these are some of the virtues reflective of true love, whether one is married, single, or celibate. Each person is called to live chastely, sexually responsible in his or her distinct vocation and life-style" (*Human Sexuality: A Catholic Perspective for Education and Lifelong Learning*, pp. 26–27).

One-Minute Scripture Retreat

Read   *"For where two or three are gathered together in my name, there am I in the midst of them."*

                                 —*Matthew 18:20*

Reflect   My child is in the process of forming his or her ideas about adult vocations. What can I do to help foster his or her discovery? What lessons from my life might help him or her?

_____

_____

Getting Started

Ask your child to share his or her first memory of doing something religious or faith-oriented. Share your own memories of his or her first questions about God.

With your child, read the second paragraph on page 35 of your child's book. Ask your child what he or she has learned about his or her own abilities by being a member of your family.

Building Understanding

Ask your child whether he or she has considered entering the priesthood or religious life, or has considered being a lay minister in the Church. Discuss with your child what he or she sees as the appeal and the drawbacks of the priesthood or religious life. Ask your child what gifts he or she has that might be useful in these vocations.

Have a discussion with your child about what your family members are doing to be signs of God's love.

With your child, discuss the *Witness Words* quotation on page 38 of your child's book. Talk about ways that your community needs to develop a Christian spirit.

Continuing to Grow

With your child, review or complete the activity on page 40 of your child's book. Talk with your child about the healthy qualities you see in him or her.

With your child, make a peace tree. On a large sheet of poster board, draw or glue cutouts of the shape of a tree with bare branches. Display the tree in a prominent place, such as on your refrigerator. Make construction paper leaves. Put the leaves and a pen or pencil in a bowl near the tree. Pray the prayer on page 41 of your child's book with your family, and invite them to write on the leaves ways that they sowed love, pardon, or any of the other qualities named in the prayer. Invite your family to continue adding to the tree for a week.

Together, look back through Chapter 4 of your child's book. Be sure to initial the HomeLink box on page 40 to show that you've reviewed the chapter, and list any questions you may have.

Read and discuss *Keep On Growing* on pages 42 and 43 with your child.

Words from This Chapter

abstinence *(p. 35):* Avoiding a particular behavior, such as the genital expression of sexuality.

procreation *(p. 35):* Participating with God in bringing new life into the world; conceiving children.

More to Share

Books

For Children

The Incredible Gift! The Truth about Love and Sex, by Keith and Tami Kiser (Our Sunday Visitor, 1996).

Helps teens understand their sexuality as a gift from God that needs to be respected and cherished.

For Adults

For Fidelity: How Intimacy and Commitment Enrich Our Lives, by Catherine M. Wallace (Knopf, 1998).

Discusses marriage and sexuality from a Christian perspective.

God's Life in Us

The Teaching Church

"Over time, the learner will develop a sense of self-control appropriate to his or her vocation in life and mature in understanding sexual morality in accord with the Church's teaching and tradition. (See *Educational Guidance in Human Love*, no. 70.) Such understanding will enable each learner to realize that the constant struggle to live in accord with the Christian vision of sexuality is sustained by divine grace, through the Word of God received in faith, through prayer, and through participation in the sacraments. Information about sexual functions and human reproduction is inextricably linked to formation in human values and Christian morality" (*Human Sexuality: A Catholic Perspective for Education and Lifelong Learning*, p. 75).

One-Minute Scripture Retreat

Read

"A thief comes only to steal and slaughter and destroy; I came so that they might have life and have it more abundantly."

—*John 10:10*

Reflect

What are the most important ways I share God's life with others? How do I experience God's life most completely?

_____

_____

Getting Started

Ask your child whether he or she thinks of himself or herself as holy. Share with your child the ways you've seen or experienced your child's holiness.

Talk with your child about the need for another chance. Share with your child a time when you were given another chance and what you learned from it. Ask your child to share a similar story from his or her own experience.

Building Understanding

Discuss with your child the commitment marriage requires. For help discussing issues related to marriage and to the breakup of marriages, see page 12 of this *Family Resource*.

Review with your child the section headed *Unfaithfulness* on page 47 of your child's book. For help discussing pornography and prostitution, see page 10 of this *Family Resource*.

Review with your child the *Stepping Stones* feature on page 49 of your child's book. For help discussing rape, child abuse, and incest, see page 11 of this *Family Resource*.

Continuing to Grow

With your child, review or complete the activity on page 50 of your child's book. Spend time together talking about problems or fears each of you might have and the resources available that may help you resolve them.

After reading together the reflection on page 51, make a "family grace" scrapbook. Ask each family member to make a scrapbook page that commemorates an experience of grace, God's life and help. Keep the scrapbook in a place where family members can add to the book in the future.

Together, look back through Chapter 5 of your child's book. Be sure to initial the HomeLink box on page 50 to show that you've reviewed the chapter, and list any comments or questions you may have.

Read and discuss *Keep On Growing* on pages 52 and 53 with your child.

Words from This Chapter

secondary virginity *(p. 45):* Used to describe the choice made by unmarried persons who have previously engaged in intercourse to abstain from future nonmarital sexual activity.

depersonalization *(p. 47):* Not acknowledging another's human dignity and rights; treating a person as an object.

pornography *(p. 47):* Material designed to elicit disordered sexual response (lust).

prostitution *(p. 47):* Exchanging sexual activity for money, drugs, or other commodities.

adultery *(p. 47):* Sexual infidelity by a married person, or engaging in sexual relations with a married person to whom one is not married.

sexual abuse *(p. 48):* The mistreatment of another person through improper sexual contact.

rape *(p. 48):* Nonconsensual sexual intercourse, often including other acts of violence; when the victim knows the perpetrator, the crime is sometimes called *date rape* or *acquaintance rape*; in some jurisdictions, even unforced sexual relations with a person under the legal age of consent may be prosecuted as rape or sexual abuse.

incest *(p. 49):* Sexual intercourse or other sexual contact between persons who are related by blood or who would otherwise be prevented from marrying each other.

More to Share

Books

For Children

The Kid's Guide to Social Action, by Barbara A. Lewis (Free Spirit Publishing, 1998).

Teaches letter writing, interviewing, speechmaking, and other skills that help teens turn ideas into action.

For Adults

Human Sexuality: A Catholic Perspective for Education and Lifelong Learning, from the NCCB (USCC, 1991).

Consolidates and updates the U.S. Bishops' position on all aspects of human sexuality—including vocations, birth control, abortion, homosexuality, marriage, and sexuality education.

Chapter 6

Life in the Spirit

Chapter Summary
- The Sacrament of Confirmation strengthens the Holy Spirit's presence in our lives.
- Christian marriage and parenting are loving and life-giving.
- Family life prepares us for living our vocation to love.

The Teaching Church

"Parents are well aware that *living conjugal chastity themselves* is the most valid premise for educating their children in chaste love and in holiness of life. This means that parents should be aware that God's love is present in their love, and hence that their sexual giving should also be lived out in respect for God and for his plan of love, with fidelity, honor and generosity towards one's spouse and towards the life which can arise from their act of love" *(The Truth and Meaning of Human Sexuality, #20).*

One-Minute Scripture Retreat

Read   *Now when the apostles in Jerusalem heard that Samaria had accepted the word of God, they sent them Peter and John, who went down and prayed for them, that they might receive the holy Spirit, for it had not yet fallen upon any of them. . . .*

—Acts 8:14–16

Reflect   How can I recognize the power of the Holy Spirit to help me foster strong, loving relationships with those who are close to me?

_____

_____

Getting Started

Talk with your child about ways your family prays together or could pray together. Ask your child to choose one new way of praying as a family to try in the coming week.

With your child, read *Acts 2:1–47* from a Bible. Share with each other how you would have felt if you had been in the upper room with the apostles. At what other times in your lives do you each feel this way?

Building Understanding

With your child, review pages 56–57 in your child's book. Discuss the rights and responsibilities that each of you have as members of your family.

Talk with your child about domestic violence. For help reviewing this topic, see page 13 of this *Family Resource.*

Role-play a family conflict. Use the steps described in the *Stepping Stones* feature on page 59 of your child's book to resolve the conflict.

Continuing to Grow

With your child, review or complete the activity on page 60 of your child's book. Talk about the ways that you feel connected to one another and how you can improve your relationship.

Ask your child to make a copy of the reflection on page 61 of his or her book. Put the reflection in a frame with a picture of your family.

Together, look back through Chapter 6 of your child's book. Be sure to initial the HomeLink box on page 60 to show that you've reviewed the chapter, and list any comments or questions you may have.

Read and discuss *Keep On Growing* on pages 62 and 63 with your child.

Words from This Chapter

domestic violence *(p. 59):* Physical or emotional violence between family members, especially spouses.

child abuse *(p. 59):* Physical, emotional, or sexual violence used by adult family members against children, or deliberate neglect of a child's physical, emotional, mental, and spiritual needs.

More to Share

Books

For Children

Bringing Up Parents: The Teenager's Handbook, by Alex J. Packer Ph.D. (Free Spirit Publishing, 1992).

Offers suggestions on how teens can resolve conflicts with their parents, improve sibling relationships, and create a happy home life.

For Adults

Annulment: The Wedding That Was: How the Church Can Declare a Marriage Null, by Michael Smith Foster (Paulist Press, 1999).

An easy-to-understand book that addresses many of the questions and misunderstandings of the annulment process in the Catholic Church.

Our Lifelong Love Story

Chapter Summary

- The history of salvation is a continuing story of the covenant of love God offers us.
- The Church witnesses to the value of growing in love.
- We will be judged on how well we have tried to love.
- The saints are role models for growing in love.

The Teaching Church

"As individual sojourners and as a pilgrim community we are called to consider, judge, and arrange our lives according to the holiness and love of God. (Cf. *Paenitemini*.) 'God signifies an alternative impulse—to sacrifice rather than grab, to love rather than lust, to give rather than take, to pursue truth rather than promote lies, to humble oneself rather than inflate the ego. In all creation, the hand of God is seen; in every human heart; in a blade of grass as in great trees and mountains and rivers; in the first stirring of life in a fetus and in the last musings and mutterings of a tired mind' (Malcolm Muggeridge, *Confessions of a Twentieth-Century Pilgrim* [San Francisco: Harper and Row, 1988], p. 67)" *(Human Sexuality: A Catholic Perspective for Education and Lifelong Learning, p. 83).*

One-Minute Scripture Retreat

Read *Therefore, since we are surrounded by so great a cloud of witnesses, let us rid ourselves of every burden and sin that clings to us and persevere in running the race that lies before us while keeping our eyes fixed on Jesus, the leader and perfecter of faith.*

—*Hebrews 12:1–2*

Reflect What have I learned about myself from this program and from my child that has improved my ability to run the race before me? What can I do to increase my ability to show my love to others?

_____

_____

Getting Started

Share with your child a recent situation in which your ability to love was challenged. Ask your child to share a situation in which he or she felt challenged to love.

With your child, look at the picture on page 65 of his or her book. Share with your child as much as you know of your family's history in the Church. If possible, call or visit older family members and ask them to share memories of family Baptisms, First Communions, and weddings.

Building Understanding

If you have a favorite saint, share the story of this saint with your child. Borrow a book on the lives of saints from the library, and read about some of the saints with your child. Together, choose two or three favorites.

Describe to your child a time when your actions had an effect—either good or bad—that you did not expect. Ask your child whether he or she has ever been surprised by the consequences of his or her actions.

Ask your child to list all the works of mercy that he or she has done today. Review your child's list, and add any act of mercy that you noticed but your child did not list.

Continuing to Grow

With your child, review or complete the activity on page 70 of your child's book.

At a family meal, read aloud the reflection on page 71 of your child's book. Ask each family member to share a way that he or she is working for a better future.

Together, look back through Chapter 7 of your child's book. Be sure to initial the HomeLink box on page 70 to show that you've reviewed the chapter, and list any comments or questions you may have.

Read and discuss *Keep On Growing* on pages 72 and 73 with your child.

Words from This Chapter

Works of Mercy *(p. 67):* Traditional lists of actions to meet the physical and spiritual needs of others.

More to Share

Books

For Children

Coming of Age: Traditions and Rituals Around the World, by Karen Liptak (Millbrook, 1994).

Discusses the similarities and differences in the coming-of-age rituals found in many different countries and cultures.

For Adults

The Thinking Parent: Understanding and Guiding Your Child, by Anne Stokes (Twenty-Third Publications, 1993).

Offers practical advice to parents about how to see things from their child's perspective and how to balance discipline with care and advice.

Family Prayers

THE SIGN OF THE CROSS

In the name of the Father,
and of the Son,
and of the Holy Spirit.
Amen.

THE LORD'S PRAYER

Our Father, who art in heaven,
hallowed be thy name;
thy kingdom come;
thy will be done on earth as it is in heaven.
Give us this day our daily bread;
and forgive us our trespasses
as we forgive those who trespass against us;
and lead us not into temptation,
but deliver us from evil.
Amen.

HAIL MARY

Hail, Mary, full of grace,
the Lord is with you!
Blessed are you among women,
and blessed is the fruit of your womb, Jesus.
Holy Mary, Mother of God,
pray for us sinners,
now and at the hour of our death.
Amen.

GLORY TO THE FATHER (DOXOLOGY)

Glory to the Father, and to the Son, and to the
Holy Spirit:
as it was in the beginning, is now, and will be
for ever.
Amen.

BLESSING BEFORE MEALS

Bless us, O Lord, and these your gifts
which we are about to receive from your
goodness.
Through Christ our Lord.
Amen.

THANKSGIVING AFTER MEALS

We give you thanks for all your gifts, almighty God,
living and reigning now and for ever.
Amen.

A FAMILY PRAYER

Lord our God, bless this household.
May we be blessed with health, goodness
of heart,
gentleness, and the keeping of your law.
We give thanks to you,
Father, Son, and Holy Spirit,
now and for ever.
Amen.